Careers without College

Private Investigator

by *Jan Goldberg*

Consultant:

D. Trent Holman
Treasurer
Oklahoma Private Investigators Association

CAPSTONE BOOKS
an imprint of Capstone Press
Mankato, Minnesota

Capstone Books are published by Capstone Press
151 Good Counsel Drive, P.O. Box 669, Mankato, Minnesota 56002
http://www.capstone-press.com

Library of Congress Cataloging-in-Publication Data
Goldberg, Jan.
    Private Investigator/by Jan Goldberg.
      p.cm.—(Careers without college)
    Includes bibliographical references and index.
    Summary: Describes the necessary training, job responsibilities, work environment,
salaries, and job outlook for private investigators. Provides addresses for contact
information.
    ISBN 0-7368-0038-7
    1. Private investigators—United States—Juvenile literature. 2. Private investigators—
Vocational guidance—United States—Juvenile literature. [1. Detectives—Vocational
guidance. 2. Vocational guidance.] I. Title. II. Series: Careers without college
(Mankato, Minn.)
HV8088.G65 1999
363.28'9'02373—dc21   98-17215
                                                                        CIP
                                                                        AC

Editorial Credits
Kimberly J. Graber and Angela Kaelberer, editors; James Franklin, cover designer
    and illustrator; Sheri Gosewisch, photo researcher

Photo Credits
David F. Clobes, 12, 22, 27, 28, 35, 36
Leslie O'Shaughnessy, cover, 6, 14, 30, 32, 38, 41, 44
Maguire PhotoGraFX/Joseph Maguire, 16
Oscar C. Williams, 4
Shaffer Photography/James L. Shaffer, 9
Unicorn Stock Photos/B. W. Hoffmann, 11; Florent Flipper, 19; Chuck Schmeiser, 20;
    Alon Reininger, 24

Table of Contents

Fast Facts

Career Title_____Private investigator

Minimum Educational_____U.S.: high school diploma preferred
Requirement   Canada: high school diploma

Certification Requirement_____U.S.: license required in most states
                              Canada: license required

Salary Range_____U.S.: $19,100 to $67,700
(U.S. Bureau of Labor Statistics and   Canada: $28,700 to $39,800
Human Resources Development Canada,
late 1990s figures)   (Canadian dollars)

Job Outlook_____U.S.: average growth
(U.S. Bureau of Labor Statistics and   Canada: stable
Human Resources Development
Canada, late 1990s projections)

DOT Cluster_____Service occupations
(Dictionary of Occupational Titles)

DOT Number_____376.267-018

GOE Number_____04.01.02
(Guide for Occupational Exploration)

NOC_____6465
(National Occupational Classification—Canada)

Chapter 1

What Private Investigators Do

Private investigators conduct investigations. They search for facts about people, places, and events.

Investigators work on many types of cases. They may investigate people's backgrounds or try to find missing people. They may investigate crimes and gather evidence.

Investigators may work for individuals or companies. Investigators receive their cases from

Private investigators may gather evidence.

clients. Clients pay private investigators for their services.

Investigators report their findings to their clients. They also may report to the police if they find information about criminal activity. Their reports may include pictures, audiotapes, and videotapes. Investigators also may testify in court. They tell the court about facts they found during investigations and introduce evidence into the trial. Investigators use this information to prove something.

Types of Investigators

Some investigators are specialists. Specialists have a great deal of training in certain types of investigations. They may handle only one type of case.

Legal investigators specialize in court cases. They assist lawyers in preparing cases for court. Legal investigators gather and study evidence. Lawyers use the evidence investigators find to

Legal investigators specialize in court cases.

prepare their cases. Lawyers advise people about the law and represent people in court. Legal investigators also may testify about their findings in court.

Corporate investigators work for large companies. These investigators may look for information about people who may have committed crimes. Investigators may try to catch workers stealing money, stealing supplies, or using illegal drugs. They also investigate people who do not work for the companies. They try to catch these people cheating the companies or stealing money from them.

Financial investigators specialize in cases dealing with money. They may try to find funds stolen by embezzlers. Embezzlers steal money from their companies.

Financial investigators also may help courts. Courts sometimes order people to pay money to someone else. For example, people who damage other people's property may be ordered to pay for the damage. These people sometimes say they do

Financial investigators help courts by searching financial records.

not have the money. Investigators help courts by searching the people's financial records for the money.

Many private investigators specialize in insurance claims. People with insurance regularly pay money to an insurance company. The company then pays for the people's losses due to sickness, fire, accidents, or other events. People sometimes pretend to have property losses or injuries to collect insurance money. Insurance companies often hire investigators to make sure the claims are true.

Many private investigators work for stores or shopping malls. People sometimes call these investigators store detectives. Store detectives protect stores' property. They watch to stop shoplifters from stealing property. Store detectives may capture and hold shoplifters. They may call the police to arrest shoplifters.

Gathering Information

Private investigators gather information in many ways. They search databases for facts. These

Many private investigators work for stores or shopping malls.

computer files organize and store information. Many public records are stored in databases. Investigators might study these records to learn about people's backgrounds.

Private investigators also interview people to find information. Investigators ask questions to learn what people know about cases.

Private investigators search for physical evidence. This evidence can be seen or touched. For example, investigators might look for fingerprints after a robbery.

Surveillance is another way private investigators find information. Investigators do this by watching people or property from hidden areas. Investigators conducting surveillance usually carry cameras or video cameras. These tools help them record the evidence they find. They also carry radios, car phones, and binoculars. Binoculars make distant objects appear closer. They help investigators watch people or property without being seen.

Private investigators may look for fingerprints after a robbery.

Chapter 2

What the Job Is Like

More than half of all private investigators have their own businesses or work for detective agencies. Agencies provide detectives to clients.

Private investigators often have unusual working hours. They must work whenever they are most likely to learn information. Investigators may work at night or early in the morning. They may work on weekends and holidays. Investigators must work unusual hours

Private investigators must work unusual hours to conduct surveillance.

17

to conduct surveillance. They also may need to contact people who cannot be reached during regular working hours.

Private investigators usually work alone. But they sometimes work with other investigators. Investigators often team up during surveillance.

Work Environment

Private investigators spend time in their offices. They use computers to search databases. They make many phone calls to gather information.

Many investigators also spend a number of hours away from their offices. They interview people and conduct surveillance. Investigators also may talk with officers at police stations. They sometimes go to court to testify.

Investigators' jobs can be risky. People can become angry if they learn they are being

Private investigators make many phone calls to gather information.

Private investigators have good communication skills.

watched. People may not want to answer interview questions. Clients may become upset when they receive reports with bad news.

Some investigators carry handguns to protect themselves. Most do not. An investigator's main responsibility is to gather information. Most investigators usually do not need to challenge or arrest criminals. Private investigators do not have police powers.

Personal Qualities

Private investigators have several important qualities. They are curious and observant. Investigators must think quickly and remember facts easily. They also must consider many possible causes for events.

Investigators have good communication skills. Investigators learn information by talking with people. They communicate information to witnesses and clients. Investigators also testify in court and write reports.

People who want to become private investigators should not be afraid of risk. They should be persistent. They often must continue to work on cases that are hard to solve. Investigators should be assertive. Assertive people stand up for themselves and tell other people what they think or want.

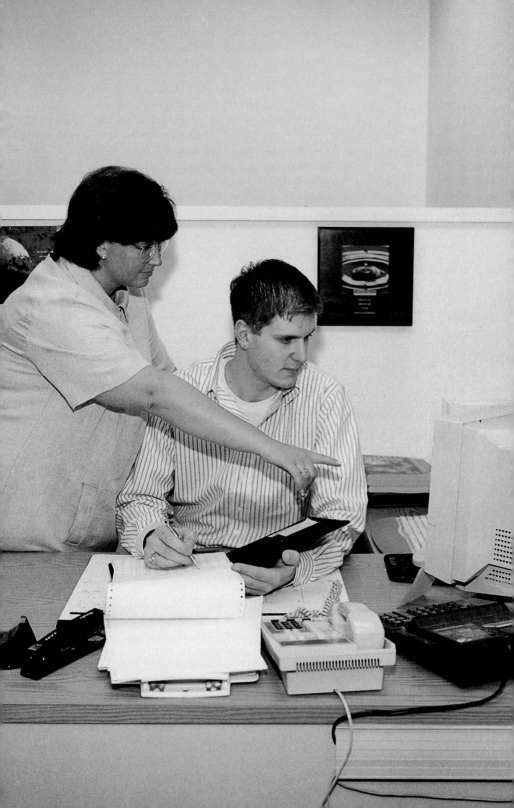

Chapter 3

Training

People prepare to be private investigators in various ways. Most employers prefer to hire people who have high school diplomas. Some companies hire people without experience to work as part-time investigators. These investigators train on the job.

The amount of education required depends on the employer. Some employers require investigators to complete programs offered by community colleges. Some investigation specialties require investigators to have bachelor's degrees,

Some investigators train on the job.

Reporters may apply their interviewing skills to jobs as investigators.

usually in law enforcement or criminal justice. People earn bachelor's degrees by completing courses of study at colleges or universities. Usually people can earn bachelor's degrees in four years.

Most investigators use skills learned in earlier jobs. Reporters may apply their interviewing skills to jobs as investigators. Many investigators learn investigative skills from military, security guard, or police jobs.

Investigators often can apply their work experience to investigation specialties. Some people become financial investigators after working in finance or accounting. Some people become legal investigators after working in law offices or on the police force.

People must prove they are trustworthy before agencies will hire them as private investigators. Applicants must pass background checks. Companies carefully check their education history and work records. Companies check for criminal records. They also check applicants' references. These people make statements about applicants' abilities.

Educational Programs

Many schools offer private investigator programs. These programs vary widely. Some involve lessons people can study at home. Others require many hours of class work. Some programs combine class work with on-the-job training.

Students in private investigator programs study many subjects. They study the law. They learn how to take pictures and interview witnesses. They learn how to spot weapons and identify criminals.

Students in other programs may study just one area. Some study criminal justice. Others study only law. Some students study business or accounting.

Licensing

Most U.S. states require private investigators to be licensed. State or local police departments usually grant licenses for investigators. All private investigators in Canada have licenses.

Investigators must meet certain requirements to receive licenses. The requirements depend on the state or province. All provinces and most states require a high school diploma. Other requirements may include background checks and written tests.

Students in private investigator programs study many subjects.

Applicants may be required to pay fees. Some states or provinces require a certain amount of work experience. Some states or provinces require investigators to continue training throughout their careers. Most states or provinces will not license someone who has been proven guilty of a serious crime.

What Students Can Do Now

Students who want to become private investigators should take a variety of classes. English classes teach students writing skills. Students learn investigative and reporting skills in journalism classes. Math and business classes teach students about finance and keeping records. Gym classes and sports help students stay healthy and fit. Students learn how to conduct research and read databases in computer classes.

People with specialized skills improve their chances of being hired. For example, a company might prefer to hire someone who can take pictures or can speak different languages.

Students learn how to conduct research and read databases in computer classes.

Chapter 4

Salary and Job Outlook

Full-time private investigators in the United States earn from $19,100 to $67,700 a year (all figures late 1990s). Average annual earnings in the United States are about $37,800. Full-time private investigators in Canada earn from $28,700 to $39,800 per year. Average annual earnings for investigators in Canada are about $35,400.

Private investigators who specialize earn more than general private investigators.

Investigators often use cars.

Private investigators can earn more money in some jobs than in others. Those who work in large cities earn more than those who work in small towns. Specialists earn more than general private investigators.

Private investigators who own their agencies bill their clients between $50 and $150 per hour plus case expenses. These expenses include motel fees and mileage. Private investigators use part of this income to pay the costs related to running their businesses.

Employers and clients usually pay for most private investigators' working expenses. For example, investigators often use cars and make phone calls.

Benefits

Investigators usually receive benefits if they work for large companies. These payments or services are in addition to a salary or wage. Investigators' benefits include paid vacations and health insurance. Investigators who do not work for large companies may not receive benefits.

Investigators' benefits also may include payments in addition to their salaries. Some companies offer profit sharing. This benefit offers employees a portion of their companies' profits. Some investigators also receive pensions. A pension is money paid regularly to a retired person.

Job Outlook

Private investigation is a growing field in the United States. The field is stable in Canada.

The private investigation field is growing quickly in the United States for several reasons. First, people are afraid of crime. They hire private investigators for protection. Second, an increasing number of people are taking other people to court. Lawyers need investigators to help them with cases. Third, a growing number of businesses are using private investigators to stop embezzlers and thieves.

New private investigators will find the most opportunities as store detectives. They also may find part-time jobs with detective agencies. Private security companies also offer good opportunities. A growing number of companies are using private security services.

New private investigators will find good opportunities with private security companies.

People who enter the private investigation field will face competition. Many people wish to become private investigators because they find the work interesting. Some people leave police and military jobs to become private investigators.

Chapter 5

Where the Job Can Lead

Some private investigators in large companies can advance. They may move into management jobs. Many private investigators stay in their jobs even when they cannot advance. Most investigators find their work interesting and challenging.

Traditional Advancement

Corporate and legal investigators advance as they gain experience. They also earn raises in salary.

Most private investigators find their work interesting and challenging.

These investigators may manage other investigators. Some oversee entire departments.

Investigators can improve their chances of advancement. They should get to know other people in the same company. They also should get to know people who hold similar jobs in other companies. These people might share information they know about job opportunities or projects. They also might suggest investigators to people who are hiring.

Investigators should be active in investigators' organizations. Involvement in these organizations will help them meet people. Contact with people in the same field will help investigators learn new ideas. These ideas may help them do their jobs better.

Investigators who have an education advance faster than those who do not. Many investigators with bachelor's degrees become managers. Investigators who know about many subjects are most likely to advance. Investigators who have

Some private investigators manage other private investigators.

specialized skills also improve their chances of advancing.

Other Opportunities

Private investigators who work for detective agencies have fewer opportunities to advance. Most detective agencies are small and offer few opportunities for advancement. Their investigators do earn salary raises. Investigators with experience often get to choose cases that challenge and interest them.

Many investigators work for stores or detective agencies when they begin their careers. They often try to start their own agencies when they have more experience.

Some private investigators move to different careers. Investigators have skills that may be useful in other fields. Related careers include police officers or government agents.

Private investigators have skills that may be useful in other fields.

Words to Know

agency (AY-juhn-see)—a business that provides a service to the public

bachelor's degree (BACH-uh-lurz di-GREE)—a title a person receives for completing a course of study at a college or university

benefit (BEN-uh-fit)—a payment or service in addition to a salary or wages

client (KLYE-uhnt)—a person who uses someone else's services

database (DAY-tuh-bayss)—computer files that organize and store information

evidence (EV-uh-duhnss)—information that helps prove something

interview (IN-tur-vyoo)—to ask someone questions

investigation (in-vess-tuh-GAY-shuhn)—a search for facts about something

license (LYE-suhnss)—a document that gives official permission to do something

pension (PEN-shuhn)—money paid regularly to a retired person

profit sharing (PROF-it SHAIR-ing)—a system in which employees receive a portion of their companies' profits

surveillance (sur-VAY-lens)—close observation of a person or place

testify (TESS-tuh-fye)—to state facts in court

To Learn More

Camenson, Blythe. *Careers for Mystery Buffs and Other Snoops and Sleuths.* VGM Careers for You. Lincolnwood, Ill.: VGM Career Horizons, 1997.

Cosgrove, Holli, ed. *Career Discovery Encyclopedia,* vol. 5. Chicago: J. G. Ferguson Publishing Co., 1997.

Goldberg, Jan. *Careers for Courageous People and Other Adventurous Types.* VGM Careers for You. Lincolnwood, Ill.: VGM Career Horizons, 1998.

Josephson, Judith Pinkerton. *Allan Pinkerton: The Original Private Eye.* Minneapolis: Lerner Publications, 1996.

Useful Addresses

Council of Private Investigators—Ontario
130 Melford Drive
Suite 8
Scarborough, Ontario M1B 2X5
Canada

**National Council of Investigation
and Security Services**
611 Pennsylvania Avenue SE
Suite 2686
Washington, DC 20003-4303

World Association of Detectives
P.O. Box 441000-301
Aurora, CO 80044

Internet Sites

Career Guide—Detective/Private Investigator
http://www.aboutwork.com/career/Careers/
   Car051.html

How to Become a Private Investigator
http://www.infoguys.com

Occupational Outlook Handbook—Private Detectives and Investigators
http://stats.bls.gov/oco/ocos157.htm

Other Occupations in Protective Services
http://www.workfutures.bc.ca/f1/
   646_EB_1.HTM

Index